WHAT WAS LEFT OF THE STARS

And some
poetry for you, too.
— Claire A.

OTHER BOOKS BY SERPENT CLUB PRESS:

WHAT WAS LEFT OF THE STARS

Poetry by Claire Åkebrand

SERPENT CLUB PRESS

WHAT WAS LEFT OF THE STARS
Copyright © Serpent Club Press, 2017

For more information please contact Serpent Club Press at editor@serpentclub.org.

Serpent Club Press books may be purchased for educational, business, or sales
promotional use. For more information please contact
Serpent Club Press at editor@serpentclub.org.

First Edition

Printed in the United States of America
Set in Williams Caslon
Designed by Emily Gasda

ISBN
9780997613445

For Michael, Isaak, and Magda

Table of Contents

First Song   1
Book of Genesis Rejects   3
Etymology   5
First Actors   6
House   7
Cain's Lullaby   8
Dusk   9
The Taxidermist's Wife   11
Waking to Crows at Night   14
Sleeping with One Eye Closed   15
Nights   16
Insomnia: 17
A Fear of Words: After Rilke   18
Ars Poetica   19
Another Ode   20
Reading *In Search of Lost Time*   21
    (Or Lullaby), (Or Trying to Remember
    How to Write a Villanelle)
Hunger in January   22
From the Crow's   23
On a Line by Wallace Stevens   24
April   25
Desire in Reverse   26
Wind's Song   27
Burning Bush   28
Outsider   29
Today   30
A Plan   31
Dinner Guest   32

Late Mercy	33
To Sorrow	34
Spilled Milk	35
A Passing Game	36
The Black Cat Crossing	37
To Be Spared	38
Faith	39
Excluded Psalm	40
October	41
Lazarus, Come Forth	42
Prayer: After George Herbert	43
As the Heavens are Higher than the Earth	44
Telephone	45
Elegy for Tomas Tranströmer	47
Smoke from a Small Flame	48
Invitation	49
From Revelations	50
The Afterlife	52
Mug Shot: Ezra Loomis Pound—May 26, 1945	53
Magpie Street	54
Lot's Wife	56
On a Photograph:	57
Night Song	58
Arrival in Hades: After Edith Södergran	59
Lullaby in a Room without a Clock	60
Silence	61
Ink Well	62
Widow	63

First Song

It can only be heard
in the most unlikely hour.
        Its tune: not as black
as the crow's
intent, nor nearly as bright
as the moon's dark side. Not sung

by night
but another voice,
older than light's first impulse
to be light,
more cumbrous

than gravity's errand.
Beyond our notes'
cages, like bells
far from any earthly tower.

And the moon, that ruin
of a ruin, who only remembers
being abandoned, circles
darkness just to hear it again.

This was someone's lullaby.
Reaching us only now—
hollow enough to hold
creation's longing.

I.

Book of Genesis Rejects

That night
Adam turned to Eve:
Let's fall
asleep under the blue
sleepless leaves.
Last time God poured sleep

over me, sleep
yielded you the way night
yields day and blue
sky, the sun, the sunfall.
But then Eve
laughed: *The sun doesn't fall. It just leaves*

the garden. Leaves
for what? Does the sun sleep,
too? There can't be any night
where sun sleeps. Adam insisted. *Blue*
Bells rise where sunshine falls.
Eve?

Have you fallen already, Eve?
The fading sun warmed the fig leaves
they didn't need to cover their sleep-
ing parts. *One long dark, before God divided night*
and day. No wonder He had the blues.
That's why He made a moon fall

3

always around the earth. The fall
moon falling even closer. Eve
stirred with night-
mares. *Go back to sleep.*
But now the leaves
kept her up. *I dreamed your lips turned blue.*

Blue
to the touch like in the eve-
ning these daisies and the shadows the leaves
make under trees. Things leap
from this darkness. Father works in the night.
Makes stars shoot. Perhaps they fall

all on their own. The night fills me with hunger. The wind blew
unknown fruit smells toward them. Eve didn't tell Adam of all
the times she'd dreamed of falling. *Sleep, while you can. Sleep.*

Etymology

The garden wanted
them out. Their awkward legs. Fingers
pointed everywhere: Over there. What is this?
Not this one. Their brand-new tongues.
Tasting berries, stone, water, vowels.

The garden wanted them
out. Their naked
hunger. Feared they'd dig down
into the deepest part—black soil
under their fingernails. Find a hidden
stream, give it a name
that could never be filtered out.

It was the garden wanted them out
in the wilderness to go till and harrow
something else. When Adam and Eve finally slunk
away, slumped over their covered parts,

the garden cowered
away in a shadowy corner
of itself and slung off all their names
like slugs. Brushed songs from its leaves
like lice. Squeezed their poison
from the serpent's mouth.

First Actors

After the last line was spoken, the last
tree disassembled, the grass carpet rolled up, and the exotic
animals backdrop folded together,
someone helped Satan unzip his serpent suit.

Adam and Eve changed into their street clothes.
She washed her face from that virgin blush,
and caught her breasts in a brassier.
He buttoned his jeans. Forced
his Sunday hair through a turtleneck.

They both fell asleep
that night tossing
in their separate beds,
hoping to be remembered
for good or ill.

House

I don't remember when we first found
the tree. Only that it curved over the brook
hidden from the playground,
and could fit us both in its hollow trunk:
You played father because you were a head
taller, your hair cut shorter. You'd pull rock
out of the brook and imagined it was bread.
We'd pretend to bake flat stones like fish, pick
at the gray flesh, and sigh and smack our lips
using lower-pitched voices to sound old.
And when we got thirsty, we'd cup and sip
the mossy air till our lungs were full of cold.
The only beds we had were our sweaters,
laid out over the dirt. But we never slept.
We were too anxious about raiding meadows
for the sugar buds of stinging nettles.
We never thought to find ourselves in the river's
mirrors. The sky broke through in some places
like rumors of adulthood, with sun slivers
through the branches' dark sieve. We'd trace
the passage of time by the growing stillness
from the playground. When was the last day
our mother called us out into the silence,
onto the pavement, into the open sky—
a blank canvas, like an empty sheet
we have to spend the rest of our lives
filling until it covers us once again like trees?

Cain's Lullaby

The shadow on the moonlit wall
doesn't know color. Who knows
if your irises will stay blue?
The light has turned.

Your closed eyelids flicker. Like leaves,
your dreams don't know words,
only noise. Your leaves haven't yellowed.
Their grip still warm on the bough.

Birds still call
unseen in you. A small wind,
almost not wind, combs through the clean,
untangled green. My son, if you dream
of me tonight—a drop of song, a note
of milk—keep me there.

Help me unlearn names
for garden, words
for falling.

Dusk

Night's tuning fork:
      half empty glass:
when violets seep
from grass
to sky:
      what brooks say in their sleep:
the sea that nightly consummates
its marriage with heaven:
              if not the ghost of our world
then of another:
             plates
set for unknown guests :
          unfurled
tablecloth:
        that is—the swallows' song
leaked into air:
          not the bread but the crumbs:
vast breathing lungs:
what came first:
        dusk or plums?
dusk or dämmerung?
            A glass half filled:
darkness spilled.

II.

The Taxidermist's Wife

Soft thuds
of Colombian butterflies
in their glass displays.
I dreamed they came to life again.

If Louis were here,
he'd groan: "Go back to sleep,"
and then blow out the candle.

But he's far out at sea.

I dreamed shells woke on the window sill,
trembling with their inner oceans;

a scraping from inside
his crates and drawers until out
thronged hundreds of dead
cicadas. I dreamed

the ibis's pink
call. A chameleon up the wall.
The crocodile's tail sticking out
from underneath the bed,
stinking of swamp.

I have called out for you
but only your Alaskan owl replies,
snow in her voice.

An unseen snake drags
its rattle through the hallway.

Bring me back something, I said,
and he brought me
from Koro Island
stones.

He strokes my hair when I'm asleep.

I dreamed his eight-hundred eggs hatched.
Not one stillborn.

I have never written him while he was away.

I dreamed the bathtub full of eels.
Their private flashing in the dark.
The splash and slosh
of wanting to live
without knowing it.

I have waited for a letter seven months.
I hate to be alone with his dead things.

The waves in the sea-
shells keep lapping,
break against my ears tonight.
Seagulls cry far away;
they haven't seen him either.

Dear Louis, I dreamed your moths unpinned
themselves and flew away.

The clatter of palm trees in the cicadas' song
flares up again.

Do you save my letters?

How does it feel to make indexes
you know will never be complete?

When he's not home, I take long walks and pick flowers.
I name them. Keep them secret.

I dreamed the jaguars
licked your bitter embalming oils
off each other.
Their breath fogged the windows.
Their deep black purrs filled me
with want.

Someone has brushed my hair
and clipped my nails.
I am propped up, made
to look like I am dreaming.

Waking to Crows at Night

Too dark to see.
Their wings like flap
boards shuffling train times, gates, names
of foreign cities. Rush
of passengers. Rustling coats
and pant legs. Steam gusts. Hiss
and slap of opening doors.

There isn't much time.
Before I can sling my hopes like a
pile of dresses into a suitcase,
the last heels fade.

Then the moon: a shattered
window in the night's station.

Sleeping with One Eye Closed

Evening climbs through the windows.
Looks us in the eyes. Wants
us to know it's there. We wait
for a word but it has nothing to say.
It moves through our spaces
like someone searching for something:
light, a corner for hiding, a greater darkness.
Rummaging through our pots and pans,
shoes in closets, our combs and soaps
in the bathroom. Lying in our beds,
we pity the night because if the plunging sky
doesn't have what the night is looking for,
no one does. We turn our backs
because we don't have it either
and if we did, we could not bear to share.

Nights

For what?
The lark's song still quivers in the trees.
And the owl with no answer
stalks a mouse across the empty field.
The owl's belly—an emptier
church—hungers for anyone
to fill its halls like alms.
Night chases fallen starlight
across its hollows.
Her starlit wings fall
toward the musky meal.
Claws boom
with impatience.

Afterwards, her call
chimes over the hills like bells:
a specific time
outside of days, nights
in which hunger
is always satisfied.

Insomnia:
Phylum Cnidaria

I kept a lion's mane in a glass jar
filled with Baltic Sea.
Gonads suspended in its bell
like bubbles in blown glass.
One day it melted into the saltwater.
Pale orange thread—unraveled.
I shook the jar and nothing
rang back.
    Colder bodies
of water spawn
infinities of others:
unfolding, deflating.
Feet of hair-thin
stinging tendrils,
dismantled harps
silently
plucking
the water.

They find
me sometimes
at night
and
burn.

A Fear of Words: After Rilke

The ease with which we name things:
this a dog and that a house.
Here is beginning and this the end.

We know everything passed and to come.
The moon rising over the mountain
can't even surprise us anymore.

How I covet that humming within things.
Everything we touch
cowers and falls silent.

Ars Poetica

Look! at the night sky—

a plundered flower shop,
its empty vases and counters.

Only the moon remains:
a shred of buttercup petal.

       And a handful of stars—
pollen scattered
            across the black floor.

Some thief in the night.
What greed, my love,

whose longing?

Another Ode

Stream, are you sure of everything
you say? Babbling away like that and all
the other things we say you do. I saw
a turtle: first dark stone,
then moving leg. Slowly it remembered
itself, and the lines of its shell
grew less precise. The night, too,
began finding its true
voice. Bluer and blacker until
actual stars. When the turtle slipped
down into your dark noiselessly:
neither froth nor ripple. The breeze—
all talk. *Branches this. Reeds that.* Couldn't show
me why any of it had to be.
It hurts me to sink
toward the stream bed
of sleep knowing exactly who
I am. Fast stream, slowing
stream, quiet brook, why
am I a person who breaks
a silence to say
fast, slowing, quiet?

Reading *In Search of Lost Time*
(Or Lullaby), (Or Trying to Remember
How to Write a Villanelle)

A mouse scurries in the attic. Outside
autumn reads convincingly in winter's voice.
The neighbor's wind-chime turns the pages

of the early cold. You stir when I turn
the page: Aunt Léonie grows old. She reads
the street outside the window. (And about

this Moncrieff translation: the French echoes
like church bells in the distance announcing some foreign
holiday or ceremony.) The lamp glows

exactly like a lamp. Silence upstairs. Something has found
what it was frantic for—the cat has stopped whining,
no longer tosses and turns

in its hunger. You turn the pages of your sleep, pause
at unknown passages. Decipher
dark. The mouse's absence turns

the pages of the attic. The pages
turn themselves. You open your eyes, a line
of milk down your chin. And amid all these pages,
was there no story? No refrain?

Hunger in January

The crows have eaten
the sky's furniture,
toppled its chairs
Scratched at its ceiling.
Picked at its wallpaper.
Winter grows
from the racket they make.

Their yack
hangs from the oak,
makes the sky swallow
its blue. Up there:
bared

bookshelves. The long
night shrivels in their cries.
(The crows are not like words across
a white page.
They devour the white page.)
They've soiled the sky's carpet. Smashed light-
bulbs and drunk

what was left of the stars
and it has not improved
their song.

From the Crow's

belly, the song
expands
in the February sky
like claws. Hangs
in trees. Smashes
against window panes—through
doors.
Picks crumbs
from the table,
my hand,
the child's mouth.

The song watches
us all morning.
Sinks in our milk
and we drink it.
Beak and bones.

The crow's song is heavy in us.
We don't know
where ours ends
and crow's begins.

We hum the tune.
We can't bear
to sing the words.

On a Line by Wallace Stevens

It is in the water of tears its black blooms rise.

I never planted them.
Not even the underworld
could have thought them up.

Night and day, they blacken the hem
of my dress as I bend over the flower bed.

The neighborhood's stray dogs
have found the hole in the fence.
They come, big and small,
at night in great salivating packs
and eat the black petals, stem and all,
howling under the moonlight.

Soon the black flowers grow back.
I continue to water them.
Or else what would become of the dogs?

April

Cherry blossoms. Warbling. Daffodils. Short
sleeves. But not everyone's smitten, not all convert
to joy's gospel right away. The grieving sort,
if there are such people, want to hurt
a little while longer. They seek more
fitting company—a cathedral
of power lines—a time before
this easy ooze of light—a winter smell
that still says: *Come, I was just mourning out
all the days of my life.* They seek groves in parks
that harbor low shadows, where doubt
is not easily lifted by the plashing larks
and their song. Swamp's heart plunges from
dark to dark: *Where I am, you cannot come.*

Desire in Reverse

A woman in a dress flutters
across a bridge on the first warm evening
of May. Mosquitoes inject

her bare arms
with her own blood,
before they fade, writhing
into their eggs.
Poppies close their lips.

A toad drops
backwards into the sky's
reflection on the pond, rings
of water shrink
back to stillness—
the toad has not yet
lusted after wings.

Wind's Song

My distant cousin : the river. Our languages
differ enough. We can't speak to each other.

In the morning, the cracked
clay pot in the garden, the toppled chairs.

Don't curse me, I've
been restless

(since the first time Eve's hair fluttered)
to find the one

thing that will return my touch. I pray,
sleepwalking among drifting leaves.

Burning Bush

Trying to keep track of a bleating flock,
stopping sometimes as if homesick

for a brother or sister, he couldn't
bear the silence, so I spoke to him. He bent

down and searched my glowing
leaves with wonder. I explained "burning

but not burning." He removed his shoes.
I tried to tell him that I was

only what I was, but a man in despair
will see God everywhere.

Outsider

The desert sky begs
to be contained,
                             it booms
through the air like sadness, over the burned fields.

It crowds
                       into the only tree around,
        the dead oak's crown,
demands to be grasped,
                         hid, framed.
But that old tree can't hold a sky.
                             The blue leaks
in and out of the pale
                 ribcage of branches.

The sky is the frame.
God made nothing bigger.

Today

It sits outside the door:
a tired dog
from who knows where.

I feed the dog.
It is always
hungry. I don't know

if love keeps
it sleeping on the porch
or just some animal instinct;

if its master had been kind
or severe. Only that the dog drags
a wild smell with it.

Its tail will wag at the
door years after my steps
no longer creak on the floor.

Some other idiot
will fill its bowl.

A Plan

(To hide a sorrow in a dusty crater
of an unnamed planet.
                    Within the most unvisited corner
of a dormouse's sleep.

Better to roll it into a bottle, lose
                    it to one of the colder seas.

Because a sorrow should never
          be completely lost. But years later
for someone to find it.

                    Who doesn't speak the
                    language.

Who would love it
for its existence, solely
          for its turning up from far away.)

Dinner Guest

When we aren't looking,
sadness tries on the face
of happiness.
Swipes its cheekbones with blush.
Slips into its clothes and turns
and turns and turns in the mirror,
glides its hands over the smooth pants,
(they are a little loose)
the round shirt buttons, the seams of the sleeves
under the armpits and along the waist.
Straightens the collar.
Ties the shoe laces in double knots.
Combs its hair. Parts it on the other side.

So that when we see sadness this way,
we wave it toward us, open all the doors,
saying the time is just right,
make a place for it at the table, fork and knife,
a porcelain plate with blue leaves along its rim.
And fill and refill its glass.
We introduce it to every one of our children.
Tell stories about blurry ancestors
in album after album.

And when the night finally pours
through the windows and the children begin to yawn,
we draw out our goodbyes, linger in doorways,
in the driveway, by the mailbox, on the street.
The children don't come to say goodbye.
Forgive our sleeping children, we say,
forgive them. They don't know who you are.

Late Mercy

On autumn evenings, bird
song is nothing but a handful
of rusty coins trickling into our open palms.
We pocket as much as we can
because we have waited
for something all year.
It will buy exactly nothing.

The coins make a sad jingling
that lasts into the winter months
in which every night, we sit around the table
having to break the news
to our slack-eyed hopes,
that they have to go to bed
hungry again.

To Sorrow

My own humming-
bird, you siphon my nectar
all through the warm months.
A long beak made to drink deeply.

You're not expected to live beyond the first year,
but sometimes survive over a decade.

At more than fifty flaps a second,
your flight looks too much
like ease.

Spilled Milk

Night pours through the kitchen window.
We have nothing new to tell each other.
In the candlelight, your hand's shadow flows
back and forth between your plate and mouth.

I don't ask about your day,
or if you, too, are afraid
that whoever holds your glass
will grow tired and turn
you upside down.
Who keeps us from spilling
at all hours from seeping
into the floorboards?

Then you spill
your milk all over the table. It widens like
a lake, drips in quick
thick drops from the tablecloth,
down the table legs,
pools at our feet.

We look down at our soaked hands and laps.
We are so relieved, we don't even know it.

A Passing Game

A February sky wants to claim it all
for itself but grief bleeds down
from the clouds, the passing bodies of geese,
and from their throats into the falling snow

from snow into the tree
tops from branches to swings from
swings to grass from grass

to looting magpies
from magpies into magpies'
indigo swipe of wings from their wings

a chair a cup a woman's cheeks a broken
comb a boot

from the cold street
to the sled
crashing down the hill.

The Black Cat Crossing

Good luck is like this,
resembling something
that used to belong to someone.
It drinks from our dog bowls,
sleeps in weathered furniture out back,
crashes through trash cans,
sends up a puff of magpies in the yard.

When it nudges open our kitchen doors,
it seems as startled as we are,
and disappears over the fence.

Sometimes growing sore and heavy,
it finds a bed of gas-stained rags
in a shed, and litters
them with hungry lives.

To Be Spared

Some nights, happiness seems as untraceable
as the call of the great horned owl
who, no matter how close, always sounds far:
> *Tonight my claws are meant for another.*
Not you. Not you.

The call chimes again in the dark
like a funeral or wedding in another valley—
and for a second one feels relieved
not to have been chosen,
until the cry fades altogether
over the fields.

Faith

The neighborhood dogs
have lost their faith,
I know it.

I said I can go on because the dogs
howl all through the night.
But they've lost their convictions.

The long black corridors
of their shouts are empty.
The moon lingers in my window, strokes

the furniture with its pale hands
like one who longs
to sit down.

The dogs used to squeal
as if at some trespasser in their yard,
a presence they sensed.

Now they bark just for the sake
of barking, to fill
the silence.

Excluded Psalm

33. The pear
bruises
before
it loses

hold.
Grains
mold
in rainy

fields.
34. Our heaven
yields
raven

after
raven. 35. If crickets
have to
forget

their lines,
if the fence
leans,
bends

to jangling
shadow,
fails at keeping
the unknown

in,
and out,
36. God, then
shout

forth
fall's spring—
Lord,
bring

us black lilies,
and ashen scilla.
37. Please.
38. Selah

October

This violet, on her way to winter months, waits
beside me at the crosswalk—

her deflated sleeves,

      her shivering waist, too skinny for that dress
so eager
            for every last
   hour of sun.

I cross, she stays.
I can't love one more dying thing.

God Almighty, might this violence
not follow me into the shadows
of my home.

Lazarus, Come Forth

He stayed
away from people
after all that.

His sister stopped asking
about those four days.
In the beginning,

she had looked at him like finally
a window,
                    a door left ajar.

But all he remembered was:
(a blind

softness, like the first
crocus of spring, roots spreading
in soil, mineral and slow),

and coming back :
petals unwrapped
toward the April
of those words.

                *

For the rest of his life,
this recurring nightmare:

A voice calling
from too far away.

Prayer: After George Herbert

The dripping faucet;
a mouse that burrows into an abandoned
house; the readiness with which blood
spills itself; the declawed cat
scratching the armchair;

crocuses bowing their heads
under snow; a stray black dog slinking
through backstreets, lapping from the gutter water,
the Milky Way;

saying please just to please the abyss;
the trunk that grows slowly through the fence;
the clothes in the closet longing for bodies,
the empty mirror for any face;

lying awake trying to remember a face
one has never seen;

the black widow dropping from the ceiling,
weaving without
light; her web's elastic wait;

the moon-stained newborn
trying out her voice.

As the Heavens are Higher than the Earth

Lord, your thoughts gather like sheep on a green hill above all earthly streams. No place to go, they lean their light heads on each other's wool, listen to one another's pulse. They are not afraid. Here, a cypress casts no shade. Nothing does. And all around them a whirr of mosquitos—bellies gorged with sweet blood. The sheep breathe deeply each other's musty smell. And that of lilies and chamomile. When sun spills through clouds, they avert their gaze. Eyelids droop and close. Lambs doze on milk, licking the corners of their mouths. And sometimes one stirs as if roused by a distant call.

Telephone

Stars whisper from one
ear of night to another.

When the message reaches us,
it is incomprehensible.

If it hadn't come so far,
we would consider this no great loss.

Relieved, we look up,
imagining the words
that might have saved us.

III.

Elegy for Tomas Tranströmer

Poems peeled
off you like bark
from a tree at the edge
of the forest,
your last blossoming twig
stolen away by a crow
into the thicker woods
where its fading cry
may as well be
an aspen's creaking.

Smoke from a Small Flame

Its grey wings spill
light across the room. No wide
open window—I don't know how it got
in. Soon it will scorch holes
in sweaters, jackets, all things wool
that easily ignite. Who lit
this flame? When these kinds
of sparks expire nothing feels
dimmer than before. The moth will
dissolve in a windowsill with the others.
Come spring, nothing but ashes.

Invitation

Spring goes out of its way:
forsythia, ranunculus, apricot blossoms.
It will even make the days longer.
And we say yes, yes, we'll come. We'll come
and we don't care why.

A summons that never specifies place or time.
We don't think to ask.

Until we find ourselves assembled together at last
in the empty ball room of winter
wondering where the chairs are, the punch bowls,
the music.

From Revelations

3. In that day, an angel will blow air
into his cupped fists. You look cold,
another will say. Remember the fire

His children used to build,
rubbing their hands like this? Back when there were nights?
Actual nights. How dark they were (or so I'm told).

And stars and moon weren't much light.
Not much at all. Though there was something about the moon.
So they said. Full of dark, cold holes. So what

made them watch it from their bedroom
windows? The way they watched trees turn green,
all those mulberries filled too soon

with worms. Back when trees had names. 4. *It had been*
so troublesome for them to recall, to guess.
And how often they got it wrong. Do you mean

they prefer these empty, nameless
streets? Empty? All things brim
with the spirit of Him who—Why does

He mind His name spoken? (one angel will ask him-
self). *If only I had one.* 5. And in that day, another
angel will drink deeply from a cup, search its bottom,

as if it had been bitter.
But there is no more bitter cup. Was it June or December
when He drank it all up? (An angel will taste the water,

roll his tongue around his mouth). *I remember*
the night I sat with Him in the garden. I like to pretend
I don't have a mind pure as jacinth, bright as amber,

and so on. 6. And the group will grow silent.
How tiresome to speak about the past
now that there's time to waste, spend

days around an imaginary feast
of bruised potatoes and chewy lamb.
7. And a trumpet will sound in the east

like an ordinary train whistle at noon. *Anyway, holy is His name.*
8. *No name can hold up against time, much less eternity.*
With God it's the same.

Yes, but holy
is His name, holy.

The Afterlife

Let day
follow
day: irises

rising
one after
another
warm
noon
after
noon

down
a lapsed
lane

Mug Shot: Ezra Loomis Pound—May 26, 1945

Speaking of apparitions—

You are the smoking bough on which the ashes of that sentence flicker.

The cracks in your face, where the lightning hit.

Magpie Street

I.

Desert town.
The crow's cry
is no shade.

*

Evening.
seagulls invent
an ocean in the air.

*

White,
but up close, the red ringed eyes
of the seagull.

II.

The pink hollyhocks
grow blue at dusk. Except
their scent.

*

Darkness:
a tailor for the hollyhock's
torn dress.

*

No night breeze.
Undressing, I pity
the frilled hollyhocks.

III.

The shadows
inside its blooms do not weigh
the hollyhock down.

*

Young pear tree.
The smell of cherries
rotting behind it.

*

The widower
grows his wife's carnations
and a beard.

Lot's Wife

Wait! she pleaded, but salt
muffled her cry. Her daughters' honey
colored hair whipped away
in the ashy breeze. *Look!*

She watched it all crumble:
stealing over-ripe figs with the boy next door;
the well she threw pebbles in just to watch them vanish;
her childhood road; the mother

who gave her a name.
What was it?

She had looked and turned
into another woman in a book.

Her name whimpers and coughs
under the rubble and wreckage.

On a Photograph:
Hiroshima in August

Mother.
Child on her lap.
Her hands around his waist
a little tighter
than in a family portrait.
Behind them
the sky still sags
with the pollen of that dusky blossom.
The city smudged from the background
like a chalk drawing—
desolate almost as the desert
that rehearsed it all.

Her hair as charred as the flaking tree
beside them, falls
across her brow and mouth like shredded curtains.
His face:
              burst window—
inside, tables and chairs
hurled to the ceiling.
Ancestors vanished
from frames in the playroom.
An upside down clock
somehow intact.

And her frown:
An entire bed swallowed by the ground
in a stripped room.
The floorboards droop
toward that hollow.

The boy is sinking
in her, too.

Night Song

The German word for light rhymes
with *nicht*. Searching definitions of light:

anything but clear.
When we sing *he is light*,

do we mean guide? Radiation
of love, or the electromagnetic kind? Light

bleaches old curtains, inspires sick skin cells to spread
like brush fire bored boys light

with broken bottles. Burnt—some will have their offerings
no other way. O, Earth, on this offense of light

turn the other cheek and carry us into a night
so dark we have to imagine the world. (Make light

all you want—) one day our lids will be drawn neatly
underground and we will long for light

in any shape: *leukos, clair, luz,*
lucifer.

Arrival in Hades: After Edith Södergran

Here is eternity's shore,
where the current rushes along
and death plays, in the reeds,
its tired old song.

Are you silent now too?
We have come from far away
and we hunger to hear—
we have never had a nurse
who could hum like you.

Lullaby in a Room without a Clock

How long have we sat like this?
Afternoon is a classroom
without noise, an empty desk, a janitor sweeping
pencil shavings from the floor.

How long will we sit like this?
Until evening? Dawn?
The hours in between

are uncombed
children kicking a moon across the night street.
They laugh only in echoes. No mothers
call them from the dark.

Silence

No words
can be spaced close enough—it lives
in the shady alleyways between letters, where mute
cats stray;

A bowl of milk, my word like a drop
of blood in it;

Silence holds me like a warm bath;

I want to brush silence's hair,
loosen its knots, the way Paul Celan groomed his quiet;

The night's twin sister.
They read each other's thoughts;

Silence sings
a lullaby to me, cradles me in the absence
of my infant's cries;

It tastes like all the words
I didn't pray;

A slow-melting night on my tongue.
I press silence's stars against the roof
of my mouth. They burn
like ice. Their light, not yet
extinct. Not yet kindled—

for now, cold stones falling
into a darkening well

Ink Well

Dusk—shadows for each object:
lamp, glass, frame.
The mortal underlined.

Bored with his work,
death falls asleep at his desk,
pen in hand,
the night, growing like an ink stain
over us.

Widow

The moon wades
       through night's swamp, knee-high
in her rags of a wedding dress,

                splotches of mud on her
                face.

From down here,
her struggle seems light.

CPSIA information can be obtained
at www.ICGtesting.com
Printed in the USA
FSHW010058310521
81864FS

9 780997 613445